T0171114

Standing in the Breeze

Prayer Journal

To you I life up my eyes,
O you who are enthroned in the heavens!
Psalm 123:1

KIMBERLY DUKES, HELEN BIBBINS

WestBow
PRESS
A DIVISION OF THOMAS NELSON

Copyright © 2013 Kimberly Ann Dukes, Helen Harris Bibbins.

All rights reserved. No part of this book may be used or reproduced by
any means, graphic, electronic, or mechanical, including photocopying,
recording, taping or by any information storage retrieval system
without the written permission of the publisher except in the case
of brief quotations embodied in critical articles and reviews.

Scripture taken from the New American Standard Bible,
Copyright 1960,1962, 1963, 1968, 1971, 1972, 1973, 1975, 1977, 1995
by the Lockman Foundation. Used by permission.

A Special Thank You to
Joshua Matthews/joshnm88@yahoo.com
for Designing Our Cover

WestBow Press books may be ordered through booksellers or by contacting:

WestBow Press
A Division of Thomas Nelson
1663 Liberty Drive
Bloomington, IN 47403
www.westbowpress.com
1-(866) 928-1240

Because of the dynamic nature of the Internet, any web addresses or
links contained in this book may have changed since publication and
may no longer be valid. The views expressed in this work are solely those
of the author and do not necessarily reflect the views of the publisher,
and the publisher hereby disclaims any responsibility for them.

Any people depicted in stock imagery provided by Thinkstock are models,
and such images are being used for illustrative purposes only.

Certain stock imagery © Thinkstock.

ISBN: 978-1-4497-9013-4 (sc)

Library of Congress Control Number: 2013905976

Printed in the United States of America.

WestBow Press rev. date: 04/05/2013

This Prayer Journey is Dedicated
To our Lord and Savior
Jesus Christ

Thank You For
Healing and Deliverance

Standing in the Breeze

Whichever way the wind blows
I'm standing in the breeze
Because I Know God will
Provide all my daily needs
All the promises of God
Are written in His Word
Just read your Bible daily and
His Voice will be heard

Whichever way the wind blows
I'm standing in the breeze
We're descendants of the promise
That's how we live with ease
Jesus is interceding for us in heaven and
God has acquitted us removed our sins our guilt
In Him only is our foundation built

Whichever way the wind blows
I'm standing in the breeze
God is not only our creator but our sustainer too
In Him everything is held together
Protected and there is no chaos
He proved his love to us by dying on the cross

Whichever way the wind blows
I'm standing in the breeze
God has never failed and is always on time
If we keep him in our lives each day
We are certain to live a life sublime
Winds will come and winds will go but
Whichever way the winds blow
God's love will forever flow

Standing in the Breeze
Prayer Journal

Presented to:

_____

*By:*_____

*On:*_____

This poem was written to uplift God and
to inspire, encourage the people of God.

Always Remember to:

Trust in the Lord with all your
Heart and do not lean on your
own understandings. In all your ways acknowledge
Him and He will make your paths straight.
Proverbs 3:5-6

Whichever way the wind blows

_____

_____

_____

_____

_____

_____

_____

_____

_____

_____

_____

_____

_____

_____

There is an appointed time for everything, and
there is a time for every event under heaven

Ecclesiastes 3:1

I'm standing in the breeze

_____

_____

_____

_____

_____

_____

_____

_____

_____

_____

_____

_____

_____

_____

_____

To you I lift up my eyes,
O you who are enthroned in the heavens!
Psalm 123:1

Because I know God will

_____

_____

_____

_____

_____

_____

_____

_____

_____

_____

_____

_____

_____

_____

_____

God is our refuge and strength, a
very present help in trouble.
Psalm 46:1

Provide all my daily needs

_____

_____

_____

_____

_____

_____

_____

_____

_____

_____

_____

_____

_____

_____

_____

And my God will supply all your needs according
to his riches in glory in Christ Jesus.
Philippians 4:19

All the promises of God

_____

_____

_____

_____

_____

_____

_____

_____

_____

_____

_____

_____

_____

_____

_____

In the same way God, desiring even more to show
to the heirs of the promise the unchangeableness
of His purpose, interposed with an oath.
Hebrews 6:17

Are written in His word

All scripture is inspired by God and profitable for
teaching, for reproof, for correction, for training
in righteous; so that the man of God may be
adequate equipped for every good work.
II Timothy 3:16

Just read your Bible daily

_____

_____

_____

_____

_____

_____

_____

_____

_____

_____

_____

_____

Be diligent to present yourself approved to
God as a workman who does not need to be
ashamed, accurately handling the word of truth.
II Timothy 2:15

And his voice will be heard

_____

_____

_____

_____

_____

_____

_____

_____

_____

_____

_____

_____

_____

_____

_____

He who has an ear, let him hear what
the Spirit says to the churches.
Revelation 3:6

Whichever way the wind blows

_____

_____

_____

_____

_____

_____

_____

_____

_____

_____

_____

_____

_____

_____

_____

_____

Let us not lose heart in doing good, for in due
time we will reap if we do not grow weary.
Galatians 6:9

I'm standing in the breeze

_____

_____

_____

_____

_____

_____

_____

_____

_____

_____

_____

_____

_____

_____

My soul, wait in silence for God only,
for my hope is from Him.
Psalm 62:5

We're descendants of the promise

_____
_____
_____
_____
_____
_____
_____
_____
_____
_____
_____
_____
_____
_____
_____
_____

And if you belong to Christ, then you are Abraham's
descendants, heirs according to promise.
Galatians 3:29

That's how we live with ease

_____

_____

_____

_____

_____

_____

_____

_____

_____

_____

_____

_____

_____

For as many as are the promises of God, in
Him they are yes; therefore also through Him is
our Amen to the glory of God through us.
II Corinthians 1:20

Jesus is interceding

_____

_____

_____

_____

_____

_____

_____

_____

_____

_____

_____

_____

_____

And He who searches the heart knows what
the mind of the Spirit is, because He intercedes
for the saints according to the will of God.
Romans 8:27

For us in heaven

_____

_____

_____

_____

_____

_____

_____

_____

_____

_____

_____

_____

_____

Therefore He is able to save forever those
who draw near to God through him, since He
always lives to make intercession for them.
Hebrews 7:25

And God has acquitted us

_____

_____

_____

_____

_____

_____

_____

_____

_____

_____

_____

_____

But you are a chosen race, a royal priesthood, a holy
nation, a people for God's own possession, so that
you may proclaim the excellencies of Him who has
called you out of darkness into His marvelous light.
I Peter 2:9

Removed our sins and guilt

_____

_____

_____

_____

_____

_____

_____

_____

_____

_____

_____

_____

_____

For you were not a people, but now you are
The People of God; you had not received mercy,
but now you have received mercy.
I Peter 2:10

In Him only

_____

_____

_____

_____

_____

_____

_____

_____

_____

_____

_____

_____

_____

So that at the name of Jesus every knee will
bow, of those who are in heaven an on earth
and under the earth
Philippians 2:10

Is our foundation built

_____

_____

_____

_____

_____

_____

_____

_____

_____

_____

_____

_____

_____

And you, Lord, in the beginning laid the foundation of
the earth, and the heavens are the work of your hands.
Hebrews 1:10

Whichever way the wind blows

_____

_____

_____

_____

_____

_____

_____

_____

_____

_____

_____

_____

_____

_____

_____

Your ears will hear a word behind you,
"this is the way", walk in it,
whenever you turn to the right or to the left.
Isaiah 30:21

I'm standing in the breeze

_____

_____

_____

_____

_____

_____

_____

_____

_____

_____

_____

_____

_____

Yet those who wait for the Lord will gain new
strength; they will mount up with wings like eagles,
they will run and not get tired,
they will walk and not become weary.
Isaiah 40:31

God is not only our creator

_____

_____

_____

_____

_____

_____

_____

_____

_____

_____

_____

_____

_____

In the beginning God created the
heavens and the earth.
Genesis 1:1

But our sustainer too

_____

_____

_____

_____

_____

_____

_____

_____

_____

_____

_____

_____

_____

_____

_____

_____

Behold, God is my helper;
the Lord is the sustainer of my soul
Psalm 54:4

In Him everything is held together

_____

_____

_____

_____

_____

_____

_____

_____

_____

_____

_____

_____

He is before all things,
and in Him all things hold together.
Colossians 1:17

Protected and there is no chaos

_____

_____

_____

_____

_____

_____

_____

_____

_____

_____

_____

_____

_____

_____

For God is not a God of confusion but of peace,
as in all the churches of the saints.
I Corinthians 14:33

He proved His love to us

_____

_____

_____

_____

_____

_____

_____

_____

_____

_____

_____

_____

_____

_____

For God so loved the world, that he gave His
only begotten Son, that whosoever believes in
Him shall not perish, but have everlasting life.
John 3:16

By dying on the cross

And Jesus, crying out with a loud voice, said,
"Father, Into Your Hands I Commit My Spirit".
Having said this, He breathe His last.
Luke 23:46

Whichever way the wind blows

_____

_____

_____

_____

_____

_____

_____

_____

_____

_____

_____

_____

_____

Come to Me, all who are weary and heaven-laden,
and I will give you rest.
Matthew 11:28

I'm standing in the breeze

_____

_____

_____

_____

_____

_____

_____

_____

_____

_____

_____

_____

We count those blessed who endured. You have
heard of the endurance of Job and have seen
the outcome of the Lord's dealings, that the
Lord is full of compassion and is merciful.
James 5:11

God has never failed

_____

_____

_____

_____

_____

_____

_____

_____

_____

_____

_____

_____

_____

And the Lord will continually guide you, and satisfy
your desire in scorched place, and give strength to
your bones; and you will be like a watered garden,
and like a spring whose waters do not fail.
Isaiah 58:11

And is always on time

_____

_____

_____

_____

_____

_____

_____

_____

_____

_____

_____

_____

_____

_____

I have been young and now I am old.
Yet I have not seen the righteous forsaken
or his descendants begging bread.
Psalm 37:25

If we keep Him in our lives each day

_____

_____

_____

_____

_____

_____

_____

_____

_____

_____

_____

_____

_____

_____

If we live by the Spirit, let us also walk by the Spirit.
Galatians 5:25

We are certain to live a life sublime

_____

_____

_____

_____

_____

_____

_____

_____

_____

_____

_____

_____

You will make known to me the paths of life;
In your presence is fullness of joy; in your
right hand there are pleasures forever.
Psalm 16:11

Winds will come

_____

_____

_____

_____

_____

_____

_____

_____

_____

_____

_____

_____

_____

_____

The wind blows where it wishes and you hear
the sound of it, but do not know where
it comes from and where it is going; so is
everyone who is born of the Spirit
John 3:8

And winds will go

_____

_____

_____

_____

_____

_____

_____

_____

_____

_____

_____

_____

_____

And let us not be weary in well doing: for in
due season we shall reap, if we faint not.
Galatians 6:9

But whichever way the winds blow

_____

_____

_____

_____

_____

_____

_____

_____

_____

_____

_____

_____

_____

_____

Devote yourself to prayer, keeping alert in
it with an attitude of thanksgiving.
Colossian 4:2

God's love will forever flow

_____

_____

_____

_____

_____

_____

_____

_____

_____

_____

_____

_____

For I have said, loving kindness will be
built up forever, In the heavens you
will establish your faithfulness
Psalm 89:2